Thibaut Meurisse is a personal development blogger, author, and founder of whatispersonaldevelopment.org.

He has been featured on major personal development websites such as Lifehack, Goalcast, TinyBuddha, Addicted2Success, MotivationGrid and PickTheBrain.

Obsessed with self-improvement and fascinated by the power of the brain, his personal mission is to help people realize their full potential and reach higher levels of fulfillment and consciousness.

In love with foreign languages, he is French, writes in English, and has lived in Japan for almost a decade.

WAKE UP CALL

Take control of your mornings
and transform your life

THIBAUT MEURISSE

RUPA

Published by
Rupa Publications India Pvt. Ltd 2021
7/16, Ansari Road, Daryaganj
New Delhi 110002

Sales centres:
Allahabad Bengaluru Chennai
Hyderabad Jaipur Kathmandu
Kolkata Mumbai

ISBN: 978-93-89967-61-6

First impression 2021

10 9 8 7 6 5 4 3 2 1

The moral right of the author has been asserted.

Printed at Thomson Press India Ltd, Faridabad

CONTENTS

PART III
How to Further Optimize
Your Morning Ritual

YOUR STEP-BY-STEP WORKBOOK

Creating a new morning ritual can be challenging, but I've created a step-by-step workbook to help you do just that. Make sure you download it by typing the following URL:

http://whatispersonaldevelopment.org/wakeupcall

If you have any difficulties downloading the workbook, make sure you send me an email at thibaut.meurisse@gmail.com and I will send you the workbook as soon as possible.

You'll also get the following bonuses:

A series of videos that I've created to help you get started with your morning ritual.

A playlist of videos that I've carefully selected to help you make the most of your morning ritual.

INTRODUCTION

WHAT YOU'LL LEARN IN THIS BOOK

This book contains a straightforward, step-by-step method to assist you in forming a new morning ritual that will support you throughout your life. I've ensured that this book is efficient and straight to the point. I want you to be able to create your morning ritual easily, rather than be weighed down with jargon in an overly long book. I've also included a comprehensive workbook as well as a morning ritual checklist to further support you.

This book is all about designing your morning ritual. I'm just here to guide you, provide information and pose powerful questions. My primary goal is to help you clarify your desire to create a morning ritual and what you want to get out of it. Last but not least, I've added concrete action steps throughout the book that will further help you create the morning ritual of your dreams.

This book will:

- Help you specify your needs to ensure you design a morning ritual that suits you.
- Provide you with a simple 10-step method to help you design your morning ritual.
- Provide you with concrete actions to take for each of the 10 steps.

- Provide you with additional resources (including but not limited to the morning ritual checklist and the step-by-step workbook mentioned earlier).
- Ensure you stick to your morning ritual through various accountability methods, such as a 30-Day Challenge and an accountability partner checklist.

I WANT YOU TO GET RESULTS

I really hope that you'll take consistent, massive action and commit yourself to creating a great and exciting morning ritual. After all, that's why you bought this book in the first place. Take action and the results will follow.

I used to be a bookworm, but over the past few years I've turned myself into a massive action taker. Why? Because I care more about results than knowledge. Don't get me wrong; I still read plenty of books and love it, but I always make sure I'm taking action every day. Knowledge is certainly power, but knowledge without action is worthless. Unless acted upon, knowledge won't bring you any real results in your life.

I strongly believe that the information in this book is powerful, but ONLY if you commit to taking action. That's why I went beyond the free, step-by-step workbook to offer a 30-Day Challenge that will guide you through the process of forming a new morning ritual. These things have been mentioned before, but I can't stress their importance enough when it comes to how much easier they will make your journey. Better still, the workbook is chock full of extra resources.

YOUR 30-DAY CHALLENGE

This challenge is pretty straightforward. At the end of the book, I'll ask you to commit to doing your morning ritual on a daily basis for the next 30 days. Don't worry, there will be more details on this, later in the book.

PART I

Why Everybody Should
Have a Morning Ritual

TAKING CONTROL OF YOUR MORNING

What is the first thing you did this morning? Did you hit the snooze button of your alarm clock? Did you complain about the weather? Did you drink your coffee hoping that it would give you an extra boost to start your day?

Unfortunately, too many people are reactive. By this, I mean that they go through life reacting to the things that go on around them often feeling powerless as a result of external circumstances. It is this attitude of powerlessness that starts their morning. They read the newspaper, which tells them how bad the economy is, how violent the world is and how prevalent terrorism is. They don't choose their attitude, they don't choose their mood and they don't set clear intentions for the day. They let everything, from the people around them to the things they watch on television, control them instead.

Regardless of your environment, the reality is that you have an incredible power to create and shape the world around you. This control starts in your mind. It always does. If you aren't priming your mind for positivity each day, you miss out on extraordinary opportunities for growth and self-actualization. In this book, we'll work on creating a morning ritual that creates sincere excitement and will, upon becoming a daily habit, have a major impact in all areas of your life. We'll work together to make sure it fully meets your needs.

ARE YOU LIVING UP TO YOUR POTENTIAL?

Most people will never reach even a fraction of their full potential. They'll remain a mere shadow of what they could have been, because they never make the conscious choice to create the life they want. They never sit down to write down what exactly they want in life. They never set clear intentions for their days. As Jim Rohn beautifully said,'I find it fascinating that most people plan their vacations with better care than their lives. Perhaps that is because escape is easier than change.'

I love this quote. Indeed, we may spend weeks or even months preparing for a vacation, be it within our country or overseas, but how much time are we really taking each year to craft our life plans? I don't know about you, but for most of us, we don't devote that much time to this.

I suspect that this has a lot to with the idea that we don't have the power to transform our lives. Unfortunately, this is a core belief that many of us have. It's something we may have been told by our parents or teachers. Or perhaps society conditioned us to believe that we have to accept things as they are and can't have what we want deep down inside. Most of us are products of our environment. If everybody around us feels powerless during our formative years, we end up feeling the same.

It never ceases to amaze me how powerless many people feel in their lives. I ran into a prime example of this recently when a 26-year-old woman earning an average salary revealed she was convinced that there was no way she could increase her earnings at any point in her life. Needless to say, she didn't believe in personal development.

I was drinking with some of my colleagues a few weeks

ago when one of them mentioned that he didn't believe in personal development. That was difficult for me to understand. If you don't believe you have any sort of power to shape your life and go in the direction you want to go, what's the point? If you think it's pointless to improve yourself and condition your mind to adopt new, positive habits, how can you expect to get anywhere in life? A lot of people seem to feel stuck where they are and see no possibilities for a better future. I don't think anyone can be truly happy living with that outlook.

In a similar vein, many people in Japan don't believe that they can become fluent in another language because they 'aren't good at foreign languages'. As a result, they think I must be some kind of genius to be able to speak Japanese so well. Yet, if you consider the fact that I've spent 10,000, if not 20,000 hours studying Japanese and have lived in Japan for many years, my ability to speak the language isn't impressive.

YOUR DAILY HABITS WILL DETERMINE WHO YOU BECOME

It's what you do each day that determines your long-term results in life. You are, quite literally, what you do and think on a daily basis. As such, adopting a few simple daily habits can have a profound impact on the amount of success and fulfillment you experience in your life. This is something that we'll continue to see throughout this book. If you look at the people that most of us consider successful, they usually aren't geniuses. They aren't fundamentally different from you. The only difference between you and them is their daily thoughts and actions, or rather their daily habits regarding what they do, what they think and what they choose to focus on. You can develop these same daily habits to support your personal goals and dreams.

THE POWER OF FOCUS

Let me start by asking the following question: What do you think about most of the time? Where is your focus during the day? We have thousands of thoughts every day, but we're largely creatures of habits. Did you know that, for the most part, over 90 per cent of the thoughts you have today are the same as the ones you had yesterday, the day before yesterday, last month, last year, or perhaps even several years ago?

The truth is, everyone has their own set of thought patterns. Yet there's one thing that all of our respective thought patterns share: They lead to a series of similar situations that continually repeat themselves. That's why some people find themselves facing the exact same relationship issues regardless of who their partner is. Do you find yourself attracting the same type of person every time you get into a relationship? If so, you're experiencing another example of the repetitive experiences our thought patterns may cause. Another example of this phenomenon is quitting a job you dislike for a new one you think you'll love, only to realize within a few months that both jobs are more or less the same.

We also go through repetitive phases. We eat healthy for a while, have a binge, return to eating healthy, and then do it all over again in a never-ending cycle. Understanding *what* you're thinking and *why* is important. In the last part of the book, we'll touch on thought patterns and limiting beliefs. We'll discuss how you can identify them and what you can do to overcome them.

Our brains share the same fundamental characteristics

and they have a fondness for running on autopilot. As a result, it's crucial to make a conscious choice to control your thoughts and focus towards what you want to attract in your life. If you don't, you'll continue having the same unhelpful thoughts you've had for years, will keep falling into the same behavioural patterns and will never be able to bring about the changes you want most in life.

As self-improvement expert Brian Tracy says, you become what you think about most of the time. He is one of the many personal development experts who espouse this belief. If your thoughts control who you'll become and what kind of life you'll have, then learning to focus on what you want to do, be and experience is one of the most important habits you can develop.

In that regard, my morning ritual has become a very effective way to focus my thoughts, stay on track with my goals, and remind me of my overall vision. I hope yours will allow you to do the same. We'll work together on creating a morning ritual that allows you to focus on what truly matters to you.

HOW I LEARNED
ABOUT MORNING RITUAL

I first heard about morning rituals from renowned motivational speaker Tony Robbins while watching some of his YouTube videos. These videos sparked my interest in incorporating a morning ritual into my own life.

Despite my interest, however, I continually failed in my attempts to create a morning ritual. I tried Tony's programme that was available on YouTube, but gave up after a few weeks. I also tried to wake up at 5 a.m. each day because it was 'what successful people do'.I failed countless times at that one, too.

I knew that having a daily morning ritual would make a real difference in my life, but I just couldn't make it stick. Looking back, I can think of several reasons why I failed each attempt.

The first reason was a lack of genuine, long-term commitment. I didn't fully commit to creating a morning ritual because I didn't take it seriously enough. For instance, I could have committed to a 30-day challenge, but for some reason I didn't.

The second reason is that my morning ritual was an example of too much, too fast, too soon. In other words, it was overly ambitious. Considering I didn't have any previous experience with morning rituals, devoting an hour a day to it was beyond what I could handle at the time. Added to the fact that I was trying to wake up way earlier than what I was used to, it was a recipe for failure.

The third reason is that I had nobody to support me and to hold me accountable during the process. Interestingly enough, I had a friend at the time who was experimenting with Tony Robbins's 'Hour of Power' series, but we just weren't keeping each other accountable. We both had great goals and good intentions, but guess what? He failed, too.

HOW I SUCCESSFULLY CREATED A MORNING RITUAL

It wasn't until the summer of 2016 that I finally managed to successfully adopt a daily morning ritual. You might be wondering how I did that, considering the plethora of failed attempts behind me. Well, it was simpler than you might think.

Long story short, I invested in a programme that focused on morning rituals, and then made a firm commitment to stick with it. I ultimately realized that the primary reason I failed in the past was that I wasn't committed enough in the first place. To this end, I discovered that investing money in a programme created a sense of dedication and the desire to take on a new habit no matter what.

I assume you want the same kind of push I did, and that this fueled your decision to purchase this book. I'd like to take the time to congratulate you on making that decision. You've taken the first step!

WHY A MORNING RITUAL
IS FREAKING AWESOME!

O nce I started to think of my morning ritual as something that would benefit me for the rest of my life, great things started to happen. I'm now happy to say that since making that commitment to my morning ritual, I've been sticking to it each and every day, apart from a few exceptions that I'll cover later in the book. Now, it's your turn! Join me and experience the benefits a good morning ritual offers.

Why bother having a morning ritual in the first place? That's a question that a lot of people ask. In this chapter, I'm going to share specific reasons why morning rituals are awesome and what you'll gain from adding one to your life.

A MORNING RITUAL ENCOURAGES YOU TO BECOME PROACTIVE

The first benefit of a morning ritual is that it increases your ability to be proactive. Instead of being like most people and reacting to whatever happens throughout the day, you start shaping your emotions as soon as you wake up. Your morning begins with thinking about your goals and reminding yourself of the bigger vision you have for yourself and the world. In essence, you're taking control of your day, your thoughts and your emotions.

This allows you to reclaim your power instead of giving it over to circumstances and events that may happen throughout the day. If you don't decide how you want to feel and what you want to accomplish each day, it's an unfortunate fact that the people and circumstances around you will do it for you. Needless to say, the people that wind up making the decision for you rarely have your best interest at heart.

A MORNING RITUAL HELPS YOU PRIME YOUR MIND

Another great benefit of having a daily morning ritual is that it allows you to condition your mind every single day in a way that suits your desires. You might, for instance, condition yourself, to feel certain emotions, such as excitement, gratitude or confidence. If you continually cultivate these emotions every day, they'll become second nature. What emotions you choose to cultivate is entirely up to you and it's almost certain that they'll change over time.

Here is an example of priming that Tony Robbins uses in his morning ritual: He immerses himself in cold water every morning. You might think he's crazy or masochistic, but he's doing that for a very specific reason. He's conditioning himself to maintain a 'do it anyway' mindset that will remove any urges to hesitate or shrink back from challenges throughout the day. As with many other things, hesitation is arguably a habit. The more you hesitate in your life, the harder it will be for you to take action. When you allow self-doubt or fear to control you, you're limited in your ability to reach your goals.

Of course, Tony Robbins knows that immersing himself in cold water is going to be painful and very uncomfortable. Yet he does it every morning without hesitation, because he understands the concrete benefits he'll gain from doing it.

A MORNING RITUAL ALLOWS YOU TO CONDITION YOUR BRAIN

Whether you realized it or not, you and I have been hypnotized, at least to a certain extent. In the book *Psycho-Cybernetics*, author Maxwell Maltz states that 'it is no exaggeration to say that every human being is hypnotized to some extent, either by ideas he has uncritically accepted from others, or ideas he has repeated to himself or convinced himself are true.'

I like to see my morning ritual as a way to dehypnotize myself from beliefs I hold and that aren't supporting me and my goals. Whether you know it or not, you're currently subject to certain limiting beliefs that determine your level of confidence, what you can and cannot do, the amount of money you can earn and the level of happiness you allow yourself to experience in your life.

Your new morning ritual will be a great opportunity to uncover some of your limiting beliefs and start reconditioning your mind to get the results you want.

A MORNING RITUAL ENSURES YOU STICK TO YOUR HABITS

Another great benefit of having a morning ritual is that it ensures you stick to your new habits every day for years to come. As you incorporate your most important habits into your daily morning ritual, you'll engage in them every day and thus maintain consistency. By stacking your habits together in your new morning ritual, you'll have a well-designed structure that will enable you to reap the long-term rewards of your new habits.

If, for example, you think meditating and setting goals are

among the things that would benefit you most at the moment, you can make meditation and daily goal-setting part of your new morning ritual and stick to that ritual for months and years to come. It's what I personally did to make sure that I took time every day to engage in the habits I believed would be the most beneficial to me in the long run.

YOUR MORNING RITUAL
IS A GIFT TO YOURSELF

I'd like you to think of your morning ritual as a gift you give to yourself each day, something that excites you as you wake up in the morning. This gift is just for you. You aren't trying to impress anybody here. It's a precious stretch of time in which you reconnect with yourself and your higher purpose while focusing on how you want to feel and who you want to become in the future.

In order for you to have the life you want and give more to people around you, it's crucial that you learn to love yourself. Focusing on personal development and spending time alone may sound selfish, but it is, in fact, one of the most selfless things you can do. It's only when you allow yourself to be happy and tap into your true potential that you'll be able to shine and have a tremendous impact on the people who come into your life, starting with your family and close friends.

Today, as I'm writing this, something quite obvious struck me: Being happy is a selfless act. If I allow myself to be unhappy, I won't be able to touch the people around me with my creativity, excitement, passion, my sense of humor, ideas and so on. I won't have the emotional resources to get out of my comfort zone and pursue my goals. I won't interact with people who could have learned something from me. My productivity will suffer, my family and friends will miss an opportunity to see me happy (and don't we all want to see our friends and loved ones happy?). It would be a no-win situation where everyone loses something.

Being happy can be a challenge and we all have times in our lives when we're feeling down, but by taking the time each day to focus solely on yourself, you can reconnect with your emotions and your deepest aspirations. After you, your loved ones will be the first group of people to benefit from your daily morning ritual.

Now, let's take a look at how you can make that gift to yourself in a way that maximizes its effectiveness and increases the impact it has upon you and those around you.

PART II

The 10-Step Formula to Create a Life-Changing Morning Ritual

In this section I'm going to provide you with a simple, step-by-step method you can follow to create a morning ritual that will really excite you.

STEP 1

CLARIFYING YOUR 'WHY'

Since you've made the decision to purchase this book, I assume that you already have certain expectations regarding your morning ritual and what you want to achieve. That said, I'd like to make sure you know exactly why you want to implement a morning ritual in your life. I'd like you to ask yourself the following question: What is my 'why'? Why do you want to create a morning ritual in the first place? Why does it mean and why does it matter?

Your 'why' will always be more important than the 'how' and 'how to' of daily morning rituals. Fortunately, it's not that difficult to grasp. Once you get clear on why you want to have a morning ritual, implementing it shouldn't be too much trouble.

For example, my biggest 'why' was that I wanted to set goals every day in a consistent manner, as I knew how important it was to set goals and how much of an impact it would make in my life in the long run. More specifically, I wanted to make sure I would spend time on my online business each day despite having a full-time job. I realized that a consistent daily morning ritual was the best way for me to guarantee that I set goals each and every day.

Another big 'why' was conditioning my brain and

changing my mindset. I wanted to spend time each morning reminding myself of my mission and the vision behind my main goals. I knew this would help me develop a powerful mindset that would support me in achieving these goals.

Our mind can be our best friend or our worst enemy. It all depends on whether we make it work for us or allow it to constantly indulge in self-sabotage. As such, it's important to realize that whether you'll stick to your habits is largely dependent upon consistently conditioning your mind to focus on what you want and believing you can achieve it. A morning ritual is a great tool for that purpose.

The 'why' behind your morning ritual might be totally different from mine and that's completely fine. In fact, it's to be expected. This is your morning ritual and what matters is that YOU get genuinely excited about it every day. It's essential that you look forward to it so that it doesn't turn into just another chore. Below are some potential 'whys' regarding your desire to create a morning ritual.

- You want to have time for yourself in the morning instead of constantly rushing through things. Perhaps you want to have a healthy breakfast or spend some time meditating.
- You want to spend some time working on a side business before going to work.
- You want to spend some time clarifying your objectives for the day and setting goals so that you feel more in control and less stressed.
- You want to exercise in the morning because attempts to go to the gym after work are marred by lack of motivation and fatigue, and often fail.
- You want to start your day on a positive note by

spending time on your hobbies or whatever else you love to do first thing in the morning.

- You want to spend quality time with your partner and/or children and create great memories together.
- You want to cultivate specific emotions or develop a powerful mindset to feel more confident, more motivated, more persistent, etc.

Action step:

Answer the following question: Why is having a morning ritual so important to you and what do you want to get out of it?

While answering this question, write down exactly what benefits you want to gain from your morning ritual using the workbook. Try to be as specific as possible.

STEP 2

GETTING EXCITED ABOUT YOUR MORNING RITUAL

Now that you've clarified your 'why', it's time to think about how to create a morning ritual that you genuinely look forward to every morning.

I understand that waking up early to spend time on your morning ritual isn't an easy task. You may not think of yourself as a 'morning person' and the mere idea that you may have to wake up a little bit earlier every day might be unappealing to you. That's why it's so important that you get genuinely excited about your morning ritual and understand the long-term benefits you'll get from it.

Let me ask you a few key questions to help you get there:

- If the only enjoyable time you could have in your day was the time you have in the morning before work, what would it look like? What would you do? How would you ensure you make the most of it?
- If you could do only one thing in the morning, what would it be? What would bring you the most enjoyment?
- If you could only feel one emotion in the morning,

what would it be? Which emotion would make the biggest difference in your life?

Remember, everybody is different and what you want to include in your morning ritual might be totally different from what other people would choose. It might even seem a bit crazy or out of the box. If so, just make sure no one's watching you.

Below are a few examples of what you could include in your morning ritual:

- Dancing to your favorite music. Now that I think of it, that's something I might like to try myself, as I enjoy dancing. One of the bouncers at a nightclub I used to go to would say, 'You're a good dancer! I always enjoy seeing you dance.' Don't tell anyone though, it's going to be our little secret.
- Enjoying a cup of your favorite coffee or tea.
- Reading books on topics that you love. If you're a bookworm like me, that might be a great motivator.
- Learning a specific skill. Perhaps you love learning foreign languages and want to spend some time studying your language of choice each morning.
- Planning your vacations or weekends. You could spend some time looking at places you want to visit in the future. Or better yet, why not read up on some of the countries you plan to visit?
- Spending time with your loved ones or doing something for them. You may want to talk to them, play a game together, or whatever else they might enjoy.
- Going for a walk. If you enjoy walking as much as I do, this is a great option.
- Spending time in silence. You could spend some time

meditating, praying, or simply enjoying some peace
and quiet.

These are just some examples. Now it's your turn to think of
some of your own!

Action step:

Write down your answers to the questions in the workbook.

What is the most exciting thing you enjoy that would
make you want to leap out of bed tomorrow? The activity
you choose will be the core activity your morning ritual will
revolve around.

Please refer to the section on waking up early at the end
of this book for more details on attaching positive emotions
to your morning and waking up excited.

STEP 3

IDENTIFYING OBSTACLES AND PREPARING YOURSELF MENTALLY

As you work on implementing your new morning ritual, you will likely face some kind of resistance. It's always a good idea to anticipate the challenges you might face and decide how you'll overcome them while sticking with your new daily habit. Chances are you've read other books and articles on morning rituals and have already tried to create your own morning ritual in the past.

With that in mind, I'd like to ask you the following question: Why didn't it work out the first time you tried to implement a morning routine? Was it a lack of commitment? Was it a lack of accountability? Was it lack of real motivation? Did you bite off more than you could chew?

Action step:

Use your workbook to write down your answers to the following questions:

- What are the reasons you gave up in your previous attempt(s)? There might be more than one. Be sure to write them all down, as it will come in handy when we work on creating your new morning ritual.

- What could you do differently this time around to ensure you stick to your morning ritual? If you've never tried to create a morning ritual in the past, just imagine things that might make you want to give up and what you can do to work around them.

STEP 4

SELECTING THE COMPONENTS OF YOUR MORNING RITUAL

The next thing you'll want to do is figure out what you're going to include in your daily morning ritual. I recommend keeping it simple in the beginning. Remember why I failed in my previous attempts? I was trying to make too many changes at once, which is always a recipe for failure.

To start, I encourage you to select one activity for each of the following areas: body, mind and spirit.[1] This includes your core activity that we previously identified. So you'll have your core activity plus two additional ones. I'll give you some examples of activities in each area. As always, feel free to choose other activities if they are better suited to your needs.

Body-related activities could include the following:

- Drinking a smoothie every day
- Taking the time to cook a healthy breakfast
- Going for a walk or run
- Stretching and/or practising yoga
- Working out

---

[1]The credit goes to Stefan Pylarinos from Project Life Mastery who came up with these categories.

Mind-related activities include the following:

- Repeating positive affirmations
- Writing down your daily goals
- Reading your list of goals out loud
- Practising gratitude

Examples of spiritual activities include the following:

- Meditating
- Praying
- Visualizing your ideal future, your best self and your life purpose

For a morning ritual that covers the mind, body and spirit, you could spend 10 minutes stretching, 5 minutes setting goals and another 10 minutes meditating.

Now, before you decide on what activities you want to include in your morning ritual, let's have a look at my morning ritual and delve more deeply into each activity. This will make it easier for you to visualize your ideal morning ritual.

CASE STUDY 1

MY PERSONAL MORNING RITUAL

Having a daily morning ritual has served me in many ways. In this section, I'll share what my morning ritual consists of and how I've benefited from it.

You'll notice that my morning ritual is constantly evolving. Below is the morning ritual I used for the first nine months of implementing it into my life. In the next chapter, I'll talk about my current morning ritual.

1. A 15-minute walk: I love walking, which is why I like to start my day by going for a 15-minute walk.

2. Five to 10 minutes of meditation: When I return home from my walk, I meditate for five to ten minutes.

3. Five minutes of empowering questions: I ask myself questions and answer them out loud. Here are some of the questions I ask myself:

- *What am I grateful for today?* We often forget about all the things we have in our lives, so this is a great question to ponder on a daily basis.
- *What am I excited about in my life?* This is a great question that I ask each day and it helps me focus on all the exciting things that I want in my life. For

me, these things include traveling around the world, learning new foreign languages, becoming a world-class life coach and writing books that will make a difference in people's lives, among other things.

- *What am I proud of?* We often take our accomplishments for granted and fail to realize how much we've already done in our lives. That's certainly true for me! Learning a foreign language, passing an exam, or losing weight aren't small feats, so why not remind ourselves of what we've achieved on a daily basis?

There are many other questions you can ask yourself. I added a list of great empowering questions at the end of this book as well as in the workbook. Feel free to ask yourself some of these questions during your morning ritual or simply create your own empowering questions.

4. Two to three minutes spent focusing on my vision and my mission: During this time, I would typically talk about my vision and overall mission out loud. It would go more or less like this, 'My mission is to inspire millions of people to create powerful habits, set exciting goals in their lives and create an extraordinary mindset that will allow them to achieve their dreams.' Or, alternatively, 'My mission is to inspire millions of people around the world to develop powerful habits and an extraordinary mindset that positively impacts everyone they come in contact with. Focusing on these things every day proved to be a great way to strengthen my beliefs and to progressively create a new reality in which I feel more confident that I'll achieve my goals. It's a great way to programme my subconscious mind and make it work for me by continually looking for more opportunities to help me achieve my goals.

5. Two to three minutes saying affirmations out loud: I like to say empowering affirmations out loud that help me overcome some of my limiting beliefs. Sometimes these affirmations were directly linked to my goals; at other times they focused on a character trait that I wished to develop over time.

My affirmation looked something like this:

- I can help anybody achieve any goal.
- I am one of the most inspiring writers of all time.
- I have absolute belief in my ability to unleash the full potential of anyone I meet.
- I'm a best-selling author who helps thousands—hundreds of thousands—and even millions of people create an extraordinary mindset that allows them to achieve their goals and live their passion.
- I'm relentless. I'm taking action all the time.
- I'm extremely wealthy because I provide massive value to millions of people around the world.
- I master my mind, which makes me unstoppable.
- There's no person, event, or circumstance in the world that can stop me from being successful.

I believe in what Muhammad Ali said: 'It's the repetition of affirmations that leads to belief. And once that belief becomes a deep conviction, things begin to happen.' I can't guarantee that all of your affirmations will become true. That said, if you repeat affirmations regarding a specific area you want to focus on, you'll start seeing a difference in your life. Your belief in your ability to make things happen will grow stronger and you'll eventually have your subconscious mind on your side. Convinced of the beliefs you've been ingraining into it, it will be able to help you attract more of what you want in life.

The key to all of this is engaging your emotions as you repeat your affirmations. Affirmations aren't just about repeating words, they're about creating experiences. Your mind has its own brand of virtual reality going on inside of it. Your subconscious mind has a difficult time telling the difference between real experiences and the experiences you imagine. This is part of why worry and expecting the worst can often lead to real-life issues. When used to your advantage, however, this is a positive thing. As your subconscious begins to believe the experiences you imagine and sees them as real, it will start to behave and act accordingly.

6. Two to three minutes reading my goals: I spend a few minutes to read my goals out loud two or three times. This allows me to focus every day on exactly what I want (my goals) and to ensure that I know what I want to accomplish this month and this year. I generally read my monthly goals as well as my major goals for the year. The more you focus on your goals, the better, and what could be better than doing it every morning? If you don't spend time to focus on your goals every day, they will likely die. If you look at people who achieve their goals, you will notice one thing about them. They are obsessed with their goals and think about them as often as they can.

7. Five minutes setting goals: I write down the goals I want to accomplish for the day. This allows me to organize my day and get specific regarding what I want to accomplish in the next 24 hours. I firmly believe that this is one of the most powerful daily habits anyone can have.

STEP 5

NURTURING YOUR BODY, MIND AND SPIRIT

The main focus of my morning ritual was setting goals and concentrating on my mission. Not surprisingly, these are the two areas in which I got the best results. By thinking about goal setting on a daily basis and reading through my long-term goals, I was able to achieve most of the goals that I set for myself in six months' time. I never imagined I'd be able to do something like that! My morning ritual ensured that I stayed on track with my goals and gave me a renewed sense of confidence that my long-term goals were within my reach. Consistently achieving my short-term goals gave me confidence in my ability to get things done. That was really exciting, because I had never experienced that level of confidence before.

The experience I've had with my daily morning ritual definitely validated my previous belief that what we choose to focus on, be it an emotion or a goal, is what we eventually end up attracting (provide we take the necessary actions, of course). In light of this, you're probably wondering why I altered my morning ritual. Don't worry, I'll discuss the reason for the drastic changes I made later in the book.

NURTURE YOUR BODY, MIND AND SPIRIT

When designing your morning ritual, you want to make sure it nurtures your body, mind and spirit, rather than just one or two of these. Let's have a more detailed look at these three things and what you can do to nurture them.

YOUR BODY

We tend to take our bodies for granted and don't think much about them when we're healthy. The minute we have a health issue however, all we can think about is healing and how badly we want to get back to having a healthy body.

Your new morning ritual is a great opportunity for you to reevaluate the importance you give to your body and your physical health. What could you do that will ensure you stay healthy? It could be something as simple as going for a walk or stretching your muscles. It could be going for a run or doing some push-ups. Or it could be having a healthy breakfast every day. If you want, it could be a combination of these things. It's entirely up to you.

As far as concrete examples go, there are two main things we can do to take care of our bodies: Eating healthy and getting exercise.

Exercising

It's a good idea to start your day with some kind of physical activity in order to wake your body up. You can run, do some stretching, take a walk, or engage in any kind of exercise that works for you.

Eating Healthy

I encourage you to include the consumption of healthy foods in your morning ritual. You could, for instance, decide to add a vegetable smoothie to your breakfast each morning or cut back on the amount of sugar that goes into your meal.

What daily habits will you implement to ensure that you take care of your body each day?

YOUR MIND

Believe it or not, your mind is the most powerful asset you have. Naturally, you have to take excellent care of it and nurture it on a daily basis. If you don't, it will become a sponge that soaks up all the negativity in your environment. You'll start limiting yourself and you'll return to the state of 'hypnosis' you were in before. You can either make the conscious choice to properly condition your mind each day by focusing on what you want and how you want to feel, or you can let society, friends, family or even strangers decide how you should feel and what you should do. It goes without saying that I encourage you to choose the first option.

It's important to understand that society as a whole can, and will always be, a pale reflection of the true potential of human beings. This is because negativity has a far more infectious power than positivity, which is largely due to the way our survival mechanisms work. We're wired to look for potential threats to our survival and thus our brains are primed to prioritize the negative over the positive. This was helpful back in the caveman era, but now that there are no sabre-toothed tigers to fend off, it does more harm than good. Another reason we tend to focus on the negative is that the 'average' person subconsciously mirrors those around them. They pick up the behaviours, beliefs and even habits of the people they interact with most frequently. Since the vast majority of people do this, it's no wonder that most of us fail to reach our true potential.

As if all this wasn't bad enough, we're constantly being told what we can and cannot do. As a result, our perspective regarding what is possible for us begins to narrow continually to the point that we wind up transferring almost all of our power to our environment.

These are just some of a variety of reasons that it's important to train your mind each day to focus on positivity. This is the best way to avoid being pulled back toward mediocrity and believing you lack the power to transform your life (which, by the way, couldn't be further from the truth!).

Conditioning your mind to focus on what you want and who you want to become is critical, and repeating this process on a daily basis is the best way to get results.

How to Condition Your Mind

There are several methods you can use to condition your mind and create a more positive mindset that will benefit you in the long run. I already gave you some examples of what I do to condition my mind, but let's go over some other ideas.

Asking yourself empowering questions is a great way to start training your mind to think positively. Check out the following examples:

- What am I excited about?
- What do I want to accomplish in my life?
- What am I proud of in my life?
- Who do I want to be 10 years from now?

- What impact do I want to have on the world?
- What do I love in my life?
- What does my higherself look like?

The purpose of these questions is to elicit positive emotions and to focus your attention on the good things in your life as well as what you want to accomplish in the future. It's important to spend time focusing on what you want, instead of the things you don't want or are afraid of.

What you focus on becomes part of your reality. Conversely, that which you ignore becomes less and less significant, regardless of its tangible reality. It may even fade from your life. Think of a problem you currently have. If you'd never had any thoughts regarding this problem, then from your mind's perspective, it wouldn't exist. The more time you spend focusing on what you want, the more likely you are to attract the results you're after. When you continually focus on what you want, the following two things will happen:

1. You'll start to believe that it's possible to get what you want, whether it's a healthy body, your dream career, the ideal partner, or whatever else you may desire. Because the thought of having these things is beginning to enter the realm of things you think are possible, you'll be less prone to self-sabotaging behaviours. You'll also be much more likely to take action towards your goals.

2. You'll become more confident and, as such, the way you talk about your goals and interact with others will change. These changes will have a direct impact on your environment and open new doors for you.

3. These things are often referred to as the 'law of attraction'. You may wonder, 'Can I really send

signals to the universe using my thoughts?' or 'Is a change in my vibrational level impacting my external environment, giving me more of what I want?'

To be honest, I don't know the answer to those questions, but that's beside the point. Whatever the answer is, continually focusing on what you want will enable you to tap into the power of your subconscious mind. It will begin to work for you 24x7, in ways that are beyond our understanding. You'll begin strengthening the belief that you can have what you want, which increases your chances of taking action and making things happen in life.

You can certainly use the so-called 'law of attraction' to your advantage and make the most of it. You're always going to attract more of whatever you focus on. With that in mind, it's important to focus on your most exciting goals and dreams.

Affirmations

As previously mentioned, daily affirmations are an effective way to condition your mind. It's best to use affirmations that are related to your goals or the traits you want to develop. If you want to increase the efficiency of these affirmations, put as much emotion as you can into them. Maintain a confident tone of voice while visualizing what will happen when your affirmation becomes part of your reality.

Let's say, 'I love being confident' is your affirmation. What does that mean to you? It might mean giving a speech with self-assurance while making eye contact with your audience. Perhaps it means speaking up during a meeting or talking to someone you're attracted to with ease. Whatever scenarios come to mind, make them as real and specific as possible.

Engaging your emotions and ensuring that your affirmation feels real gives you an amazing amount of power. The more you engage your emotions, the better this works. Did you know that many high-level athletes, chess players and pianists spend hours visualizing their moves and routines?

Our mind has the incredible power to imagine things that aren't there with enough realism that our brain can't tell the difference.

There was an experiment conducted in the 1960s that proved this very point. The experiment evaluated the ability of students to make free throws under various conditions. They were divided into three groups. The first group was asked to spend 20 days engaging in 20-minute practice sessions, the second was asked to refrain from practising, and the third was asked to spend 20 minutes imagining themselves making free-throws for 20 consecutive days.

Ultimately, the group of students who practised in their imaginations performed almost as well as those who practised in reality. More specifically, those who practised improved their scores by 24 per cent, while those who practised in their minds improved by 23 per cent. Students who refrained from both visualization and physical training showed no improvement. This experiment was conducted multiple times and continued to yield similar results.

With that in mind, just think of what will happen if you spend months or years visualizing yourself achieving specific goals or feeling certain emotions on a daily basis. Stephen Covey says that everything is created twice. In his words, 'There is a mental (first) creation, and a physical (second) creation. The physical creation follows the mental, just as a building follows a blueprint'. Personally, I would say that things are created more than twice. I believe they are created thousands and thousands of times in your mind, before they become part of your reality. What once seemed an unattainable dream becomes something you believe to be possible. It then becomes part of how you define yourself, at which point your action will begin to match those of someone who already has what you want. Over time, this closes the gap between where you are and where you want to be.

Goal-Setting

Setting goals as part of your morning ritual is another powerful way to condition your mind by writing down the goals you want to accomplish for the day. Remember that the more you focus on what you want, the better your results will be.

A GPS can only reach a specific destination if you tell it where exactly you want to go, and the same is true of our minds. The human mind is actually a powerful goal-setting and -getting machine. Yet if you neglect to tell it exactly what you want, it can't help you achieve your goals. Setting long-term goals gives you a sense of direction and setting daily goals gives you the momentum to keep moving forward in that direction. Sadly, most people lack clarity when it comes to what they want to accomplish in life and, as a result, fail to get the results they desire.

If you have previous experience with goalsetting, you've probably noticed that you tend to achieve more when you take the time to write down your goals. Now, imagine how much you could get done if you set goals every day for the rest of your life while maintaining a clear sense of direction. Within the next five years, you'd find yourself way ahead of those who aren't working on clear, written goals on a daily basis (most people aren't!). If you're committed to setting great goals and actually achieving them, I encourage you to check out my goal-setting book. It discusses the process of setting goals in detail and will show you how to set goals that you're genuinely excited about.

SPIRIT

When I say 'spirit,' I'm not necessarily referring to religion. Although religion is an important part of spirituality for some, I'm referring to your vision and life purpose. In other words, the things you believe you were born to do or are at least very excited about. I'm also referring to meditation, prayer, or anything else that quiets your mind and connects you to your best self.

Vision/Life Purpose

Most people have something they want to do in life, but the sad thing is that most of them won't do anything about it. All too often, people tell me about their hopes, dreams and goals, but they refuse to take the first step towards making these things a reality. The following quote from personal development expert Brian Tracy says it well:

> 'You might not know how you are going to achieve your goals, and you certainly don't understand what all the steps involved are, but you know the first step, and it is always crystal clear. Then, once you take that first step, the second step will uncover, and so on.'

Personally, I try not to worry too much about how I'm going to accomplish a goal I set for myself. I just set it and start taking action, with the belief that I'll eventually find a way to achieve my goal. How about you? What is your first step?

The Power of Vision

Your vision is one of your most powerful assets. With a clear and compelling vision, you'll accomplish more than some of the smartest people you know. Your vision will push you to keep going when everybody else has given up. It will also enable you to master whatever skill you set your mind to, to the extent that you'll be able to surpass people who are more talented than you. Everything you do will be influenced by your sense of purpose and your ability to see your best self. Many people just want to make a living from doing what they're passionate about. There's nothing inherently wrong with this. However, the compelling vision that you hold within you will provide a strong desire to make a difference in other people's lives. You'll want to transform society in some way, shape, or form, which lends tremendous power to your actions. In many cases, there's nothing more powerful than a compelling vision.

If you haven't yet figured out what your vision or life purpose is, let me share a few things that all great life purposes have in common.

A great life purpose should be:[2]

1. *Timeless*: If you could use a time travel machine to go back in time or travel to the future, your life purpose would remain the same regardless of the era.
2. *Universal*: You could have been born in a totally different part of the world and your life purpose would remain the same.
3. *Inspiring*: Your life purpose should be truly inspiring, allow you to unleash your full potential and experience

---

[2]From Celestine Chua's e-book *How to Discover Your Life Purpose.*

genuine fulfillment. When you're aligned with your life purpose, the work you put into it won't feel like work at all.

4. *Transcendent*: Your life purpose should allow you to transcend your ego. Most of us work to survive, gain recognition, accumulate possessions, or to feel accepted by society. A genuine life purpose comes from a place of love, not fear. A clear life purpose enables you to stop acting out of fear. Although we may not be able to eliminate our egos, we should aim to control them and act from a place of love as much as possible.

If you're still not sure what your vision or life purpose is, just think of a long-term goal that you're drawn to and would like to see happen in the next five years. Now, to ensure that you live your life in sync with your life purpose, it's important that you take time each day to remind yourself of what your life purpose is, why it matters to you and how it makes you feel. As mentioned before, you can talk about your life purpose out loud while visualizing yourself in situations that reflect it. How does that make you feel? How do you act and behave in a way that reflects your life purpose? You might also want to write your life purpose down.

Meditation

Meditation has multiple benefits and I highly encourage you to include it in your morning ritual. You can start with just a couple of minutes a day. There are as many ways to meditate as there are people; there is no 'right' way to do it. The idea behind meditation is learning to detach yourself from your thoughts and observe them rather than identify with them.

The simplest way to meditate is to close your eyes and focus on your breath. I'm not an expert on meditation so I'm not going to go into too much detail here. If you want to learn more about meditation, I highly recommend purchasing a book on the topic and trying various methods until you find what's best for you.

Prayer

Praying is another way to nourish your spirit and you don't necessarily need to be religious to experience its benefits. For instance, you could pray for the well-being of your family and friends. You could also express gratitude to God, the Universe, or whatever force resonates with you for everything you have in your life. Prayer can be used as a way to celebrate how blessed you are.

Action step:

Use the workbook available to write down a detailed description of what your morning ritual consists of.

STEP 6

DECIDING HOW MUCH TIME YOU HAVE AVAILABLE

The fifth step is deciding how much time you want to spend on your morning ritual and each of the activities included in it. Your morning ritual can be as short as 10 to 15 minutes, 30 minutes, or even an hour or more. Personally, I would start with at least 15 minutes a day, but half an hour or more is preferable. As I'll explain in the last section of the book, you can always choose to dedicate more time to your morning ritual later on if you desire.

Action step:

Write down in the workbook how much time you'll dedicate to your morning ritual, breaking it down by activity.

STEP 7

REMOVING ROADBLOCKS AND DISTRACTIONS

As you start performing your morning ritual, you'll want to make sure that it goes as smoothly as possible. The last thing you want is to spend 5 minutes looking for your running shoes or 10 minutes looking for the perfect relaxation video on YouTube. It's distractions like these that could lead to self-sabotaging behaviours and potentially diminish the effectiveness of your morning ritual. By making sure you prepare everything you need the night before, your morning ritual will become easier to maintain.

In addition, the evening preparation process will become its own ritual that will further condition your mind and strengthen your commitment to your morning ritual over time.

You could, for example, prepare your running gear the night before so that you can go out for a run first thing in the morning with minimal thought and effort. This makes it easier to head off any excuses that your mind may think of to skip your run. Or you could make room on your desk for a piece of paper or a journal you can use to write down your goals, what you're grateful for, or whatever else in your morning ritual that involves writing.

Tip: Make sure that the first thing you do in the morning is part of your morning ritual. It's easier to maintain a morning ritual if the first thing you do upon waking is a part of it.

Action step:

Write down what specific things you'll do to make your morning ritual 'intuitive' and as easy to maintain as possible.

STEP 8

SETTING YOURSELF UP FOR SUCCESS

You can make your morning ritual even easier to implement by preparing for it in the evening. It goes without saying that the quality of your morning ritual is closely linked to what you do the night before. For example, a poor night's sleep will negatively impact your ability to perform your morning ritual and could ultimately ruin it.

GETTING ENOUGH SLEEP

I've seen and heard many people say that the amount of hours you sleep per night doesn't matter as much as we might think. They feel that a person's energy levels are more about their mindset than about how long they sleep. They believe people who are excited about their morning rituals and set intentions to wake up feeling energized can sleep less.

I can't say I agree with this. Your mind is certainly powerful enough that, with sufficient training, you may be able to significantly reduce the amount of time you spend sleeping. After all, the monks of Mount Hiei, Japan, walk the equivalent of a marathon every day in addition to cleaning their temple, all on just four hours of sleep. This takes an incredible amount of training, however, and I highly recommend sleeping at least six hours each night to avoid feeling exhausted when you wake up.

My morning ritual allowed me to function on less sleep than before I started it, but scrimping on sleep for long periods of time isn't a good idea. Try to give your body as much sleep as it needs. That said, we all have times where we don't get enough sleep and wake up tired, so I'm going to give you a tip that may help in that situation. Repeatedly telling yourself how tired you are is one of the most common urges when this happens, but it creates unnecessary mental suffering and makes you feel even more exhausted than you already are. Repeating something negative to yourself throughout the day, even if it's rooted in truth to some extent, will only make you feel worse about the situation. It may even make the situation itself worse.

If you happen to get less sleep than you usually do, conserve your energy; just don't spend energy reminding yourself how tired you are. Train yourself not to think about it and go about your day.

SETTING INTENTIONS THE NIGHT BEFORE

Setting your intentions for the day ahead is a great way to prime your mind and improve the quality of your morning ritual. For instance, you can rehearse your morning ritual in your mind and get revved up for it. You can decide what emotions and benefits you'd like to get the next morning.

In addition to that, you can also create a small, evening ritual that mirrors your morning ritual. Your mind is very suggestible before you go to sleep and it is thus a great time to set intentions for the next day. If your focus is on feeling happier and more grateful for what you have, you could listen to gratitude affirmations, or you could repeat your own affirmations before going to sleep.

Now it's time to discuss what you can do to increase your chances of getting a good night's sleep.

IMPROVING THE QUALITY OF YOUR SLEEP

There are many ways to improve the quality of your sleep, so let's go over some of them.

- *Make sure your bedroom is pitch-black.* Many studies have shown that the darker the bedroom is, the better we tend to sleep. If your room isn't pitch-black, what could you do to make it darker? Maybe you could buy a sleep mask or curtain that does a better job at blocking the light in the morning.
- *Avoid using electronic devices.* This applies to smartphones, tablets, televisions and the like. According to SleepFoundation.org, 'Careful studies have shown that even our small electronic devices emit sufficient light to miscue the brain and promote wakefulness. As adults, we are subject to these influences and our children are particularly susceptible.' A 2014 study published in PNAS (Proceedings of the National Academy of Sciences) has shown that melatonin, a chemical that helps regulate our sleep patterns, was reduced by 50 per cent in participants who read with electronic devices rather than books.[3] These participants took about 10

---

[3]Chang, A. M., Aeschbach, D., Duffy, J. F., & Czeisler, C. A. (2014). Evening use of light-emitting eReaders negatively affects sleep, circadian

minutes longer to go to sleep and lost 10 minutes of deep sleep (also known as rapid eye movement [REM] sleep). Participants also reported feeling less alert in the morning. If your device has a light setting for nighttime use, it may still have a negative impact on your sleep, but just test it out and see if it makes a difference. If you absolutely have to use electronic devices at night, consider wearing glasses that block the blue light they emit. It's best to put the glasses on a few hours before you go to bed.

- *Relax Your Mind.* If you're like me, you may have all kinds of thoughts running through your mind when it's time to go to bed. I tend to get very excited about new ideas I have or things I want to do. As a result, I often feel like there are so many things I could've gotten done during the day, and these feelings make it difficult to sleep. Aside from turning off electronic devices before bed, I've found that listening to soothing music really helps. Reading a physical book can help me relax as well (as long as I don't get too excited by the book, which has been known to happen!)

- *Avoid drinking too much water within two hours of going to bed.* This one is obvious, but still worth mentioning. If you have to go to the bathroom in the middle of the night, it's going to interrupt your sleep patterns. This, of course, will probably make you more tired the next day.

- *Have an evening ritual.* This alone will help you fall asleep more easily. It's best to try going to bed at the

timing, and next-morning alertness. *Proceedings of the National Academy of Sciences*, 112(4), 1232-1237.

same time every day, including the weekends. If you like to go out during the weekend and stay up late, this will be hard to do, but I encourage you to give it a try and see how it goes. An evening ritual will also help you stay on track with your morning ritual. It will be easier to wake up every day at the same time without feeling tired if you go to bed every night at the same time. If you do go out and stay up late during the weekend, one thing you can do is to still wake up early as during the weekdays and have a couple of naps throughout the day when necessary.

ADDITIONAL TIPS:

Stop using horrible sounds for your alarm clock. I use my smartphone as my alarm clock and, up until recently, the sound I was using to wake up was terrible. Why on earth would you want to hear a sound that pisses you off or frightens you first thing in the morning? It doesn't make sense, but it's what most people do (including me for quite some time).

It's much better to wake up with a sound you really enjoy, a sound that you associate with positive emotions. If your alarm clock sound sucks, you might want to change it. More specifically, choose a sound that you wouldn't mind listening to during the day. Better yet, choose a sound that you would actually enjoy listening to during the day.

FINAL TIP

You can work on associating your alarm clock sound with positive emotions by using it throughout the day in a positive setting. For instance, you could use the sound for your alarm clock as a timer when you meditate in the morning.

If you have difficulties sleeping well, try to implement some of the things mentioned above. The best advice I can give you is to keep trying different things until you figure out what works for you. We should all be our own scientist because what matters in the end is not what studies say, but what you experience and how you feel. In the last section of this book, I'll go into more detail about what you can do to wake up earlier each day. You can also purchase devices that track the quality of your sleep. They'll show you how much time you spend in different sleep stages, so you'll know whether you're getting enough quality sleep (especially deep sleep). I haven't done this myself, but it's something I'd like to do in the near future. I'm definitely curious about my quality of sleep.

STEP 9

COMMITTING 100%

As I mentioned in the introduction of this book, one of the reasons I failed to stick to my morning ritual was that I didn't fully commit to it. Please avoid my mistake. I know that if you stick to your morning ritual for long enough and start seeing its benefits, you'll likely keep it for many years.

I haven't been 100 per cent consistent with my own morning ritual and I'm certainly not perfect by any stretch of the imagination. That said, when I decided to commit to it, I was able to stay with it long enough to understand its benefits. My ability to do this stemmed, in part, from the fact that I had a long-term perspective. I wanted to keep that morning ritual for decades to come, maybe even for the rest of my life.

I have no intention whatsoever of getting rid of my morning ritual. I do, however, plan to change it as needed. I want to continually optimize my morning ritual to get the most out of it and achieve my goals. At the same time, I want to cultivate a deeper sense of gratitude and fulfillment for the things that I already have in my life.

Now it's your turn to commit to your morning ritual and to give it 100 per cent. We're going to discuss how to do just that in the upcoming section.

UNDERTAKING THE 30-DAY CHALLENGE

Now that you've written it down, I'd like to encourage you to undertake a 30-Day Challenge to strengthen your commitment to your new morning ritual.

My goal is to help you get through the challenge, and the workbook is one of the many ways I'll support you throughout this challenge.

Are you ready to embark on the 30-Day Challenge? The fact that you're still reading tells me you are!

You'll find your '30-Day Challenge Pledge' at the end of the workbook. Be sure to fill it in and sign it.

To further show your commitment, you can send me an email at thibaut.meurisse@gmail.com with a simple 'YES', or (better yet!) with a 'YES' *and* a description of what morning ritual you are committing to.

Action step:

- Commit to the 30-day Challenge by filling in the 30-Day Challenge Pledge.
- Send me an email to let me know you're in. You can say 'Hi' to me while you are at it!

STEP 10

CREATING ACCOUNTABILITY

Many people invest a sizeable amount of money in coaching and a big reason for this is that they need accountability in order to make sure they follow through with what they said they'd do. If you aren't confident enough in your self-discipline and are afraid of getting off track, you should strongly consider finding an accountability partner to help you stick to your new morning ritual.

To help you do that, I've created an Accountability Partner Checklist. Feel free to use it if you decide you need someone to help you stick to your morning ritual. Although the checklist is part of this book (in fact, we'll be going over it soon), you'll also find it in the free workbook that comes with this book.

Action step:

Use the checklist to find an accountability partner who will help you stay on track.

ACCOUNTABILITY PARTNER CHECKLIST

To ensure that you perform your morning ritual every day, it's best to find an accountability partner. Below is a guideline you can use to help you find one and maintain a supportive relationship with him or her.

Contact your soon-to-be accountability partner and give them the following information:

What Your Morning Ritual Consists of

- What are the components in each category (body, mind and spirit).

What Specifically You're Committing to

- Commit to your morning ritual by telling your partner what you're doing without any room for guesswork or ambiguity. Say 'I commit to doing my morning ritual every day for the next 30 days, which means I'll do A, B and C for X number of minutes.'

Why It Matters to You

- Why is your ritual important to you? What consequences will you face if you don't perform your morning ritual every day?

How You'll Communicate Your Progress

- Will you be using emails, phone calls, texts, in-person meetings, or a combination of all four?
- How often will you communicate your progress?

What Will Happen If You Succeed? What Will Happen If You Fail?

- What will the reward for succeeding be? How do you plan to treat yourself and further encourage your commitment if you succeed?
- What will the punishment for failure be? Perhaps you'll bet money on your success and give it to your accountability

partner if you fail, or maybe there's another consequence that you feel works better.

ADDITIONAL TIP

You could send an email to your accountability partner every day letting them know you've completed your morning ritual. How's that for commitment?

KEY POINT

Make sure that you're as specific as possible and that your accountability partner is someone who understands the importance of your new morning ritual and takes it seriously. Obviously, the more disciplined they are, the better. After all, we're only as good as the company we keep.

Now it's time to look at a few things you can do to continually optimize your morning ritual. For simplicity's sake, I'm going to use my personal experience as an example. Although everyone's experiences are different, there are some core elements that apply to all of us.

PART III

How to Further Optimize
Your Morning Ritual

Your morning ritual should be something you want to do every day for years to come, or perhaps even for the rest of your life. As the months, years and decades pass however, your needs will evolve along with your goals and aspirations in life. Your morning ritual needs to evolve with them. Even if you stayed exactly the same for the rest of your life, having the same old routine day in and day out for years on end would eventually become boring.

This is why it's important to view your morning ritual as a flexible routine that can be adjusted over time. It can be revamped to suit your needs as you go through different periods of your life. It isn't some rigid routine that stays stagnant your entire life.

In this section, we're going to explain how you can take your morning ritual to the next level and continue to improve it so that it serves you well in the long run. I recommend going through the 30-Day Challenge before you work on optimizing your morning ritual, and you certainly don't want to tweak it if you find that it's still working for you.

TAILORING YOUR MORNING RITUAL

TAILORING YOUR MORNING RITUAL TO ACHIEVE YOUR GOALS

You implement your morning ritual because you want to achieve a specific goal. This goal could be personal, professional, or emotional. Maybe you want to create an online business like I do, or you want to advance your career. Or maybe you want to strengthen your relationship with your partner.

Whatever your goal may be, you can allocate more time to focus on the task that will help you the most when it comes to achieving that goal.

As an author and blogger, writing is the task that will help me most when it comes to achieving my goals. It's easier said than done. Even so, I dedicated 45 minutes each morning to writing blog posts and books after I'm done with my morning ritual.[4]

Action step:

Answer the following question: What is the one activity that, if done on a daily basis, would be most helpful in achieving my goal?

---

[4]See case study 2 below for more information.

ADJUSTING YOUR MORNING RITUAL

As time passes, your goals and aspirations are going to change. You may have achieved one of your goals and are about to move onto the next one on your list. As we mentioned before, there's great power in focusing on what you want, but what do you do once you've achieved your goal? Your only option is to focus on your next goal, right? Doing this means adjusting and tweaking your morning ritual over time so that it's in line with what you want to accomplish and how you want to feel.

CASE STUDY 2

MY NEW MORNING RITUAL

Let's take a look at my new morning ritual. As of this writing, I've been at it for a few days. Before we do, however, I have a confession to make. I mentioned that I've been doing my morning ritual every day since June, aside from a few exceptions. That exception happened to be about a month ago, when I skipped it for almost a week.

There were a few reasons for this, but the biggest one was that my morning ritual had become too repetitive and mechanical. I was also dealing with a great amount of dissatisfaction with my job, which left me feeling dejected and demotivated, to say the least.

Up until then, the main focus of my morning ritual had been thinking of my goals and writing them down. While this has helped me achieve several goals in the past few months, it also led to focusing too much on the future and neglecting the present.

I realized that I needed to shift the focus of my morning ritual to enjoying the present moment, which led me to make significant adjustments and spend more time on meditation and gratitude exercises. It's still a work in progress, but here's what my new morning ritual looks like now:

- *10 minutes of meditation first thing in the morning*, before my mind has a chance to become cluttered. This makes for a more enjoyable meditation session. In short, I lengthened the amount of time spent on meditation.

- *Five to 10 minutes of stretching while listening to gratitude affirmations.* I've found it more effective to listen to some affirmation soundtracks on YouTube than to ask myself what I'm grateful for. That may change over time for me and you might feel the opposite is true for you. That's fine; it's precisely why we tweak our morning rituals.

- *Five minutes reading my gratitude journal and writing new entries.* I started a journal a couple of years ago in which I wrote every positive comment people made about me. It could be something a friend told me, a positive review for one of my books, positive feedback regarding my blog, etc. I hadn't used this journal for a while, but it's been incorporated into my revamped morning ritual. Lately, I find it helpful to reread and add to it.

- *Five minutes repeating affirmations related to happiness and asking myself why being happy is so important.* Consciously or subconsciously, we often block our own happiness for various reasons. It could be because we feel it's wrong to get too happy when so many people are suffering in the world. It could be because of our past or things we don't like about ourselves. Sometimes, it's because we've attached certain conditions to our happiness, like being in a relationship, having a certain career, or having the perfect body. Personally, I find it very useful to reframe my perspective on happiness by redefining it as the most selfless thing there is. After all, you can't help others if you're miserable. I also try to focus on all the benefits that happiness brings. Below are some of the affirmations I've come up with:

1. I give myself total permission to experience peak levels of happiness throughout the day.
2. I allow myself to be ecstatic, experience joyfulness and make the most out my day.
3. I have the absolute right to be happy and to enjoy my life to the fullest.

I also spend some time delving into how happiness benefits me and those around me. Being happy allows me to be more creative, inspired and motivated. It also gives me the courage and emotional strength to step out of my comfort zone. It allows me to be healthier and have a more positive impact on people around me. The list goes on and on. There are so many reasons to be happy, but we can easily miss them if we focus on the wrong things.

- *Five minutes setting my daily goals.* This is something I did with my previous morning ritual, so there's been no change in this department.
- *10 to 15 minutes of reading personal development books.* I read books related to personal development or coaching to put myself in a good mood.

I'm giving you all these details because I want you to realize that your morning ritual is not set in stone, and that it can, and should, be continually improved and adjusted to reflect your evolving needs. I also wanted to show you that, when you have a long-term vision and think of your morning ritual as something you want to keep for the rest of your life, you'll be able to stick to it. Even if times get tough or you skip it for a few days, you'll be able to keep on going and recover from any setbacks.

WARNING: Avoid skipping your morning ritual at all (reasonable) costs, especially during the first few months. After that, you'll have received enough benefits from it that you'll realize that it's something you want to maintain for a long time.

Action step:

What could you do to further optimize your morning ritual?

USING YOUR MORNING RITUAL TO OVERCOME YOUR LIMITING BELIEFS

Your morning ritual is also a great opportunity for you to overcome your limiting beliefs. In this section, I'm going to talk more about what limiting beliefs are and how you can identify and overcome them.

We all have limiting beliefs and mental blocks that prevent us from experiencing deeper levels of fulfillment and success in our lives. This is where your new morning ritual comes in handy. Indeed, now that you have a daily routine, you can spend some time each day overcoming your limiting beliefs while creating new, empowering beliefs that will better serve you in your future.

It's important to realize that, in the end, no belief is inherently true. This means that neither your limiting beliefs nor your empowering beliefs are true, either. What it all comes down to, then, is how you want to play this game called 'life'. Do you want to believe that you're totally confident and can become world class at anything you set your mind to? Do you want to focus on strengthening that empowering belief every day? Or do you want to believe that you're unworthy and will never achieve any of your goals? The outcome of the game isn't decided by outside forces, it's actually decided in your mind, whether you're conscious of it or not.

I can't recall the number of times my mind has played tricks on me that undermine my efforts. It's clear to me that the ability to overcome self-sabotage is what will allow me to achieve the goals that truly matter to me. This, of course, will enable me to create the life that I want. Believe it or not, this applies to you as well. You're probably sabotaging yourself in some way right now. You may have beliefs that prevent you from experiencing more happiness, creating more wealth, or achieving goals that are important to you.

It might seem as if you go two steps forward, then one or two steps backwards, constantly sabotaging your efforts. If so, it's crucial to identify your limiting beliefs and work on eliminating them. This is the only way to stop yourself from going through life with your breaks on and to start giving more to the world around you. As a friend of mine once said, 'It's time to come out of your shell, shed your fears and share more of yourself with the world'.

HOW TO IDENTIFY LIMITING BELIEFS

Have you ever talked yourself out of something you wanted to do? Why did you do that? Chances are, you did it because you have some fears or beliefs that made you think you couldn't do it. Someone else could, sure, but not you. This is a perfect example of a limiting belief. Or rather, a belief that prevents you from doing what you want.

You can start identifying your limiting beliefs by looking at each area of your life, one by one. As you do this, ask yourself the following questions: If I had what I wanted in this area, what would that look like? What's preventing me from reaching the ideal situation in that area? Why am I not yet where I want to be in that area?

Here are some of the areas you might want to explore:

- *Personal Growth*: Do you feel like you're growing and utilizing your full potential?
- *Finances*: Do you often worry about your finances? Do you have the lifestyle you want?
- *Career*: Do you enjoy your job? If you had to work until your last breath and couldn't retire, would you want to continue with the job you have now?
- *Health*: Do you feel tired and sick or do you feel energetic and healthy?
- *Family*: Do you have strong bonds with your family or support system? If not, how could you strengthen these bonds?
- *Relationships*: Are you happy with the relationship you're in? Is there anything that's missing?
- *Social Life*: Do you have meaningful interactions with other people? Are you happy with the amount of time you spend socializing? If you're an introvert, you might want to spend more time alone. If you're an extrovert, you might long to socialize more.
- *Attitude*: Do you feel like you have the right attitude and mindset, or is there room for improvement?
- *Contribution*: Do you feel like you're contributing to something meaningful? It could be through your career, relationships, or other activities such as volunteering.

By asking yourself these questions, you'll come across some disempowering beliefs. Below are some of the most common ones:

- I'm not smart enough

- I'm not good enough
- I don't deserve it
- I don't have the resources I need
- Money is the root of all evil

HOW TO OVERCOME YOUR LIMITING BELIEFS

The beliefs that are holding you back weren't created out of thin air. They're all artificial beliefs that you've accepted on some level, be it consciously or subconsciously. In fact, most of the disempowering beliefs you hold were accepted by you subconsciously during childhood. In his book, *Secrets of a Millionaire Mind*, T.Harv Ecker explains that most of us have a money blueprint that is similar to that of our parents. For instance, if your parents consider money as the root of all that kills, it's likely that you'll hold negative beliefs regarding money. If you don't 'like' money, how can you possibly become wealthy?

These negative beliefs can manifest in different ways. You might consistently sell your products or services at a low price, thus preventing you from enjoying the level of wealth you desire. Or you might lose your money in 'unexpected' ways when you exceed a certain amount. Once you understand your personal money blueprint and are able to change it to attract more wealth, your finances can change dramatically. This is just one example of how your beliefs create your reality. To learn more, you can check out my article '4 Disempowering Beliefs about Money That Keep You Poor'.

Once you've identified the major limiting beliefs you want to get rid of, you can use various techniques each day to get rid of them.

The first thing to understand is that beliefs are created through repetition. In fact, that's how propaganda and even cults work. Something that is repeated enough times will eventually be accepted by our subconscious mind as true.

Getting rid of your limiting beliefs means exposing yourself to things that counter these beliefs. This has to be done on a regular basis. You have to take the time to ask yourself what makes the limiting belief untrue. Look for as much evidence as you can. You can also utilize the following techniques:

- Affirmations
- Visualization
- Constant exposure to counterexamples through books, videos and other mediums
- Surrounding yourself with people who, in social circles, hold the beliefs you want to have

Action step:

Do the exercise above and identify limiting beliefs in each area by asking yourself why you aren't already where you want to be.

Create one or two affirmations that you believe will help you overcome your limiting beliefs.

Find books or people that could help you shift your beliefs.

WORDS OF CAUTION:

Limiting beliefs can be deeply ingrained in your subconscious mind, so it may take months or even years before you're able to overcome some of them. This process will require delving deep within yourself and being brutally honest. It may not be easy, but remember that there's no belief that is inherently true and that applies to your negative belief, no matter how deep-seated it is.

HOW TO WAKE UP EARLIER

As you decide to dedicate more time to your morning ritual, you'll probably consider waking up earlier. But how do you do that? In this section I'll give you some practical tips to help you wake up early each day while maintaining your morning ritual. You don't want to wake up at 5 a.m. just because it's 'what successful people do'. If that's your primary reason for doing so, I can pretty much guarantee you'll fail.

The first obvious question that you want to ask yourself is: Do I really want to wake up earlier? If so, why do I want to wake up earlier?

The only way to wake up early on a consistent basis is to have a strong reason to do so. That sounds obvious, but it's often overlooked. If your 'why' is weak, you won't succeed. Think of it as a basic formula that goes as follows:

Desire to wake up early < Pain of waking up early = Failure

In other words, your desire to wake up earlier has to be greater than your desire to sleep in.

No matter how much you think you *should* wake up earlier, it won't happen if you don't *feel* you should wake up earlier. We're emotional beings and we need to appeal to our emotions if we want to wake up earlier or add any other change or habit to our lives.

There are countless reasons why you may want to wake up

early and you'll succeed if these reasons are important to you. Let's take a look at the two things that will have the biggest impact on your ability to wake up earlier.

1. *The emotions you attach to waking up early.* This includes your 'why' and any emotions you attach with waking up earlier. Perhaps you feel a sense of being in control of your day, maybe you get excited as you work on your side business, or maybe you enjoy being able to spend precious time with your partner or children. It could simply be the positive feelings you get from taking time for yourself. Whatever it is, attaching positive emotions to waking up earlier will make it easier to do so.

2. *The approach used.* As I mentioned before, if you start waking up earlier in addition to creating a morning ritual that's loaded with new habits, you're going to feel overwhelmed. Feeling overwhelmed is a stepping stone to giving up. It's much better to start with a simple morning ritual and get used to it before adding anything major. Once your morning ritual becomes second nature, you can dedicate more and more time to it and start waking up progressively earlier. To avoid feeling overwhelmed, you might decide to wake up one minute earlier each day. That would be 30 minutes early after a month, and one hour early after just two months! Does waking up one minute earlier tomorrow than you did today sound like an impossible task? I have a feeling you think it's pretty easy to do.

Once you get your emotions and approach right, waking up earlier should be significantly less challenging.

MORNING VS EVENING

Now, let's take a deeper look at the emotional benefits you attach to both your mornings and your evenings.

It's important to understand that the size of the gap between how you feel about your time in the evening and your time in the morning has a lot to do with how difficult it will be for you to wake up early. If you love watching movies on Netflix at night, but find yourself waking up late and rushing to get to work or school on time, you probably hate getting out of bed in the morning. Chances are, you don't want to cut your evenings any shorter, either.

Just take a few seconds to ponder the following question: What emotions do you attach to your morning? Are you excited to wake up tomorrow morning or do you dread it?

Now, consider the following questions: What emotions do you attach to your evening? Are you excited to watch your favourite TV show on Netflix or read your favourite book? Are you looking forward to eating dinner with your friends or spending time with your family?

Evening		Morning	
Activities I currently engage in	How do they make me feel?	Activities I currently engage in	How do they make me feel?
• Watching movies • Reading • Spending time with my friends/loved ones	• Watching movies • Relaxed • Loved	• Watching movies • Going to work	• Watching movies • Stressed

The more excited you get about your morning ritual, the easier it will be for you to go to bed early. This, of course, will make waking up earlier far less difficult.

The good news is that, no matter where you stand right now, the fact that you bought this book already tells me that you have a certain degree of motivation and some solid reasons to wake up early in the morning. You just need to figure them out and weigh them against your reasons for staying up late.

To that end, I'd like you to try this exercise. Take a sheet of paper, or preferably, refer to 'Waking Up Early' from the downloadable workbook. Then write down things you enjoy doing in the evening on the left and the things you enjoy doing in the morning on the right. Once you're done, write down the emotional benefits you get from each activity. See the example below:

Evening		Morning	
Problems I experience	Consequences	Things I would enjoy	Benefits
• Watching too much TV • Spending too much time on the Internet • Playing too many video games	• Feeling guilty, wishing I had used my time more effectively • Losing respect for myself • Feeling progressively less confident	• Reading my favourite book • Exercise • Drinking coffee while listening to music	• Contentment • Energy • Feeling relaxed • Feeling excited to work on my goals

What you've probably noticed is that you currently derive more pleasure from your evenings than your mornings and that you don't have much to look forward to each morning. What we're going to do now is recalibrate your evening and morning, so that your morning is much more pleasurable.

This is what you have to ask yourself: What would I need to do in the morning to get as excited as I do about the evening?

To further help you, fill in the table from the section 'recalibrating your morning' that you can find in your workbook. (see example below)

My guess is that these exercises gave you a better understanding of why it's hard to get excited about your mornings. You may be associating evening with pleasure and morning with pain right now, but it doesn't have to be that way. That's just how you've conditioned your mind in the past. It can be changed to better suit your needs and goals. How you want to feel when you wake up and what you want to get out of your morning is entirely up to you.

I hope you now have more clarity regarding why you want to wake up early. Maybe you know you want to get up early, but you still can't motivate yourself. If so, try waking up just a little bit earlier each morning and take it one day at a time. Eventually, you'll adjust to waking up earlier and get a chance to see the potential benefits.

Many people tend to be more productive in the morning. This is due in part to the fact that most people who wake up early do it with a purpose in mind. As a result, they start doing something as soon as they get up. Most people don't wake up at 5 a.m. to watch a series on Netflix, waste their time watching cat videos on YouTube, or play video games excessively. It's certainly possible for someone to do that, but it's highly unlikely.

At the end of the day, deciding to wake up earlier is your decision. It may not be something you want to do right now, but find yourself drawn to in the future. As always, experiment, see what works best for you and remember that you can make changes whenever you need to.

THE IMPORTANCE OF BEING CONSISTENT THROUGHOUT THE WEEK

One of the final things I'd like to cover is the importance of consistency. If you decide to wake up early, you have to do it every day of the week, including weekends. I know this may sound difficult and it probably will be in the beginning. If you wake up early every day however, you'll quickly adapt to it. As such, it will become easier and easier each day.

On the other hand, if you wake up earlier during the weekdays but stay out all night and wake up at 2 p.m. on Friday, Saturday and Sunday, Monday morning will be tough. The whole week might be tough, for that matter!

Just bear in mind that, if you're truly committed to waking up early, you'll get way better results by staying consistent. If you happen to go out late, you can still wake up early and take naps throughout the day to avoid disturbing your rhythm more than you have to.

CREATING A MORNING RITUAL THAT YOU LOOK FORWARD TO (MY PERSONAL EXAMPLE):

In conclusion, I'd like to return to my morning ritual to further illustrate the point I've been making. I'm not a morning person and I like to spend my evenings either working on my business or reading books. I always wish I had more time in the evening and often wound up going to bed late because of that. I'm not particularly excited about going to work, either, which is another reason I tended to go to bed late. It was a form of escapism.

As you can imagine, this ended up creating a vicious cycle where I became increasingly tired and demotivated by my job. Needless to say, motivating myself to wake up early wasn't easy under those circumstances. Waking up earlier and redesigning my morning ritual has done a lot to help me break free of that cycle.

I realized that I needed to build up excitement and attach more positive emotions to my morning ritual if I wanted it to benefit me. I've started shifting my beliefs by considering my morning as a sacred time that I wanted to cherish. I've begun to feel that, no matter how boring or tough my day may be, I will have had my morning to spend on the things that matter most to me.

I've started asking myself how I can create a morning ritual that really excites me. What is it that I need most right now? In asking that question, I discovered that I needed to focus on feeling more grateful, allowing myself to be happy and living in the present.

In the past several weeks, I can honestly say that I've been looking forward to the morning more than I ever have before. I like the feeling of having time to focus on my goals, plan my day, read books or articles about personal development and, most importantly, focus on writing. I've gone from dreading getting up in the morning to go to a job I don't enjoy to looking forward to waking up every morning.

If you want to create a great morning ritual that you're excited about, it's totally possible. Even if your life is far from where you want it to be, you can give yourself the gift of taking some time each morning to focus on the things that matter to you. In short, you can give yourself time to start improving your life with each passing day.

TAKE ACTION RIGHT NOW, OR ELSE...

The usefulness of the information I've given you all depends on what you choose to do with it. Act on it and it will become empowering. Do nothing and it will become random information. At best, its biggest benefit will be your ability to give friends and family tips on creating a morning ritual. You won't have one yourself however, and that's the most important thing. I've been there myself. I've been that person who knows all sorts of information, but has never put it to use. Needless to say, that doesn't create the results you want in your life. So, take action today!

After releasing my book on setting goals, I received comments from people who told me that it made a real impact on their lives. These people put the book's contents to use and turned the knowledge they received into tangible results. To my delight, one of my readers took immediate action upon reading my book:

> 'I myself have a lofty goal that I have only just begun to work on, and after reading this book, I stopped everything and used the steps to lay out a plan for not only how I am going to accomplish this, but when.'
> Mark Richmond, US

Another reader began to impact others by sharing the book with her kids:

'Your book has been an inspiration in my life and I want
to thank you. I'm halfway through your book and I want
to give to my kids as well.' – Kelly D.

It goes without saying that I would love to hear more stories
like that from my readers.

So, who do you want to be—the person who invests in
themselves and gets results, or the person who doesn't value
themselves enough to take consistent action?

EMPOWERING QUESTIONS

'Quality questions create a quality life. Successful people ask better questions, and as a result, they get better answers.'

—Tony Robbins

Here is a list of empowering questions you can use every day during your morning ritual. I recommend answering these questions out loud while visualizing what they mean to you. The more you can engage your emotions, the better. Try them out and choose the ones that resonate most with you.

GRATITUDE

- What am I grateful for?
- What am I taking for granted that I once dreamed of?
- What am I taking for granted that I could be grateful for?
- Why is my life such a blessing?
- What brings me joy in my life?
- How is my life better than I think?
- What have I already succeeded at?

FEELING GOOD ABOUT YOURSELF

- What do I love most about myself?
- What makes me feel proud of myself?

- What skills do I have that make me proud of myself?
- What character traits do I have that make me proud of myself?
- What have I done that I'm proud of?
- What challenges have I overcome that make me proud of myself?
- Who makes me feel good?
- What's the best part of my personality?
- What makes my life amazing?
- How do I want to feel today?
- How could I choose to feel today?
- How can I maintain a positive attitude?
- What positive emotions could I allow myself to experience at a higher level?

GETTING EXCITED

- What do I do well?
- What would I like to learn to do well? What can I do to make this happen?
- What gets me truly excited about life?
- What could I do to make my life even more amazing?
- What is my life purpose? If you don't know, ask 'What might my life purpose be?'
- What motivates me to do my very best?
- What am I truly passionate about?
- Right now, at this very moment, what do I want most? What will I do to get it?

EXPLORING YOUR POTENTIAL

- What does success look like to me?
- What's the one thing that I haven't done, but really want to? What am I waiting for?
- What could I be the best in the world at?
- What do I want more of in my life?
- What kind of person will I be in one year, five years, or 10 years from now?
- What would I do today if I were to act like my future self? How would I behave? How would I feel? What would my confidence levels be?
- What would my future self like me to do, believe, or experience right now?
- What would my future self say to me today? How would he/she encourage me?
- What could I do today that would make 'future me' proud?
- What self-limiting beliefs have I been clinging to?
- How would my life improve if I got rid of this belief?
- How did 'future me' overcome this self-limiting belief?
- What can I do that I'll enjoy while stepping out of my comfort zone?

COMMITTING TO YOUR GOALS

- What is my number one goal in the next six months? What enables me to achieve it?
- What am I committed to in my life?
- Who do I need to become to achieve my goals?

HEALTH

- How can I create a healthy lifestyle?
- How can I take better care of my body?
- Why is having a healthy body important to me?
- Why do I want to respect my body?

RELATIONSHIPS

- How can I strengthen my relationships with my loved ones?
- How can I experience more excitement and joy in my relationship with my partner?
- How can I surprise my partner today?
- What could I do that would make my partner's day better?

CONCLUSION

I would like to thank you for purchasing this book and also to congratulate you one more time for having reached the end of it. You've already shown more commitment and determination than most people. Now, I have no doubt in your ability to successfully create an exciting morning ritual that you can stick to. But does that mean everything will go as planned? Well, if there's one thing I've learned in life, it's that things rarely go as planned. If you fail in your attempt to create a morning ritual, don't blame yourself. Remember that I failed several times myself. Pick yourself up, reread this book and give it another shot. There are few things in life that can't be overcome with perseverance, so keep trying!

If you have any questions, feel free to contact me anytime at thibaut.meurisse@gmail.com. I'm not going anywhere! I'm on my own journey towards improving my morning ritual as well as my life in general. I hope we can keep growing together.

I'll leave you with a quote I came across while reading motivational speaker Steve Pavlina's blog:

> 'In the long run, people usually do achieve their goals if they persist, stay flexible and don't give up. The biggest challenge for most people is persisting long enough to win the mental game.'

I wish you all the best and I'm looking forward to hearing from you soon.

Thibaut Meurisse